In the Cave

Felicity Hopkins

Oxford

1   The picnic

This is the story of two children. They were brother and sister and their names were Catherine and Alex. Catherine was eleven and her brother was eight.

It is also the story of some dark caves.

It was summer. Catherine and Alex were not at school. They were with their grandfather and grandmother on their farm.

The farm was not near the town. It was quiet and there were lots of trees and grass. The children liked it. Grandfather and grandmother had hens, ducks and cows. They had a dog too. His name was Biff. Catherine and Alex liked Biff. Biff liked them.

It was Monday. It was the first day of the holiday. It was ten o'clock and the sun was high in the sky. There were no clouds. It was a beautiful day.

'Come here, Biff,' shouted Catherine. 'Good dog. We are going to the hills.'

Biff was very happy.

'Do you want any apples?' said grandmother. She was in the kitchen.

'Yes, please,' said Catherine. 'Alex, please help grandmother. You can put the food in the bag.'

Outside it was hot. Biff walked in front, smelling the ground. Catherine was second with the bag. Alex was last. There were trees next to the path. There were lots of red and blue flowers under the trees.

They walked for a long time. At twelve o'clock they were at the bottom of the hills. There was no wind. It was very hot.

'I want a drink,' said Alex. 'I want some food too. Can we have our picnic?'

'Yes,' said Catherine, 'but it is very hot here.'

'We can go in there,' said Alex and he pointed to a hole in the side of the hill. It was behind some tall trees.

'It is a cave,' said Catherine. 'We can eat our picnic there.'

The children liked the cave. It was clean and light, but it was not hot. There was sand on the floor.

'Put the bag here,' said Catherine. 'We can sit on these stones.'

'I like it here,' said Alex. 'I can bring some toys here. We can put them behind these stones.'

'Yes,' said Catherine, 'it is our picnic cave. We can put wood across the front and we can play here. Do not tell grandfather or grandmother. Do not tell anyone.'

For the children it was a game. They did not know it was the start of an adventure.

2 Where is Biff?

In the afternoon the two children played games in the cave.

'Look,' shouted Alex, 'there is a hole at the back of the cave. It is full of stones but there is a small hole at the top. Can I climb up and look?'

'Be careful,' said Catherine. 'Do not fall.'

Alex climbed to the top and looked into the small hole.

'I cannot see,' he said. 'It is dark in there.'

Catherine and Alex went to the cave again the next day. It was Tuesday.

'We are taking Biff to the hills,' they said to their grandmother.

This time they put a torch in the bag.

Catherine climbed the pile of stones and she looked into the small hole at the top.

'I can see now,' she said. 'It is another cave. I am shining the torch on the ceiling, but I cannot see the bottom. We can move some stones and make a bigger hole. Then we can see.'

'Can we go in then?' said Alex.

'I do not know,' said Catherine.

The children worked for a long time. There were a lot of stones. They were very heavy. Alex and Catherine were careful. Now there was a bigger hole.

'We can go in the cave now,' said Catherine. 'Please hold the torch for me.'

Catherine climbed over the last stones. She put her foot on the floor of the cave. There was water. She put her hand on the wall. There was water there, too. She climbed into the cave.

'Be careful,' she said. 'It is wet. Do not fall. Hold my hand.'

Alex climbed over the stones. Biff was last. He did not like the water and he was not happy. He had his tail between his legs.

The two children looked at the cave. It was small—smaller than the picnic cave. It was colder too and very quiet. The hole was behind them. Through the hole was the picnic cave. Outside there were birds. There was grass. It was a hot day. Here there was no sun. It was dark and wet.

'Is it dangerous?' said Alex.

'I do not know,' said Catherine. 'I do not like it.'

'Where is Biff? Is he with you, Catherine?'

'No,' said Catherine. 'I do not know where he is.'

'Biff,' they shouted. 'Biff, Biff.'

He did not come.

They shouted again. Catherine looked through the hole. He was not in the picnic cave. Where was he?

They shouted and shouted.

'Come here, Biff. Good dog. Biff. Biff.'

3 In the dark passage

'Look,' said Catherine. 'There. Give me the torch, please.'

In the middle of the wall was another hole. It was the start of a passage and there was Biff.

'It is not very high,' said Catherine. 'I can touch the ceiling with my hand. We can go inside. Biff can walk in front.'

The passage was different from the wet cave. There was not any water on the walls and the floor was dry. But it was dangerous. The children walked and their shoulders touched the walls. Their clothes got dirty.

'Where is it going?' said Alex.

Then there was a loud noise. Alex fell down. Catherine dropped the torch and it was dark.

'What is that noise?' Catherine shouted.

She picked up the torch. Alex was on the ground.

'My ankle, my ankle,' he said.

Catherine looked. There was red on his sock.

'It is not a bad cut,' she said. 'But look. You kicked a pile of small stones. And what is this?'

In her hand was a bone. It was old and brown. Alex looked. Biff sat down. More stones dropped to the floor. There was another bone. The children did not like it.

'What are these bones?' said Alex. 'Is there something bad in this cave?'

The passage was small and dark. Where did it go? Was it empty? The children listened. There was nothing. In front of them it was black. Behind them it was black. They looked into the circle of yellow light from the torch. Then they saw something. They saw two eyes. Two fires in a dark, animal face.

4   Help

The animal face looked and looked. The eyes did not shut. The children looked too.

'It is a picture,' said Alex. 'Who painted it?'

Then there was a noise. It was not loud but the children heard it and Biff heard it too.

'Biff is running away,' said Catherine. She shouted but it was no good.

'Come back,' she shouted again.

'I can catch him,' said Alex.

'Wait,' said Catherine. 'Do not run. It is dangerous. We are going home now. We can catch Biff outside.'

Then they heard the noise again. This time it was louder. They walked along the passage and into the wet cave. But where was the hole to the picnic cave?

'Shine the torch,' said Alex.

There was the water on the floor and the walls were wet. It was the right cave but in front of them was a big pile of stones.

'That was the noise,' said Catherine. 'It was these stones falling. What can we do? The stones are very big.'

There was a small hole at the top. A small window of light. Catherine climbed up.

'It is no good,' she said, 'I cannot see.'

'Can we shout?' said Alex.

'Yes, but there is nobody outside. We did not tell grandfather or grandmother. They do not know where we are.'

'What can we do then?' said Alex. 'We cannot stand in this water. My feet are cold.'

'Don't cry, Alex. Don't cry. Listen. It is Biff. He is outside. He is in the picnic cave.'

Catherine climbed up again.

'Biff,' she shouted, 'Good dog. Come here.'

Biff climbed up on his side. He put his nose through the small hole. His tongue was wet on Catherine's face.

'Listen,' she said. 'Go to the farm. Tell grandfather. Tell grandmother. Bring them to the cave. Go back to the farm, Biff.'

The children waited in the passage. It was dry there. They had some bread and two apples in the bag, but not blankets or coats. They were cold.

They waited and waited. Catherine went back to the wet cave and climbed up on the stones. There was no light through the small hole. It was night.

In the morning Alex was asleep on her shoulder. Then they heard grandfather and the men.

5   The story of the cave

The story was in the newspapers.

'Look,' said grandfather. He had a newspaper in his hand.

The children looked. It said CHILDREN FIND CAVE PAINTINGS. There were pictures of Catherine and Alex, of grandfather and the men, and of Biff.

Lots of people went to the caves. They went along the passage with big torches. There were more paintings. Clever people talked about them and wrote about them.

It was on television too. Doctor Vickers talked about the pictures and the cave.

Dr. Vickers The cave is very old. People were there a long time ago. They painted the animals on the walls.

T.V. Man How many pictures are there?

Dr. Vickers There are forty-two in the passage. The children were only at the start. It is a very long passage.

T.V. Man The children say there was a pile of stones in the passage.

Dr. Vickers Yes. That is right. They were not stones. They were hammers and knives made of stone. People used them for cutting meat or for making clothes.

T.V. Man The children say there were animal bones there too.

Dr. Vickers Yes. You can make a knife from a bone. People used small bones for needles.

'Lunch,' shouted grandmother.
They sat down at the table.
'What are you doing this afternoon?'
'Can we have a picnic?' said Catherine.
'Yes, but do not go into any caves,' said grandmother.
They all laughed.

The true story of the Caves at Lascaux

There are cave paintings in many different countries. In 1940 four boys found the paintings in the caves at Lascaux in France. They were with their dog. Now these caves are very famous.

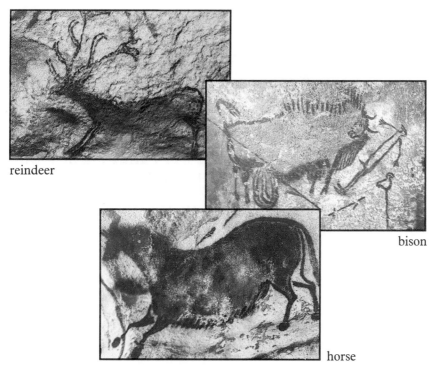

reindeer

bison

horse

People painted the pictures 30,000 years ago. There are lots of different animals. Some of the animals are different from the ones we have now. There are bison, horses and reindeer. These animals were food for the people.

Why did people paint the pictures? We do not know. They did not live in the caves. It was difficult to paint the pictures. It was very dark in the caves. They had lamps. The lamps did not make the caves dirty. There was no black smoke.

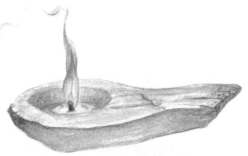

The paintings are on the walls and ceilings of the caves. The ceilings are very high. They put wood across the caves and climbed on it and painted the ceiling. Some of the pictures are very big. One picture is five metres long.

The people had three colours—black, red and yellow. They used black for the outside of the animals. They used a stick to draw the lines. They put red and yellow inside the black lines. The paintings are very beautiful.

Questions and exercises

1 The picnic

1 What were the children's names?
2 Was the farm near the town?
3 Did grandfather and grandmother have a cat?
4 What was their dog's name?
5 Did the holiday start on Wednesday?
6 Was the first day of the holiday hot or cold?
7 Did Biff like the hills?
8 Where did Alex put the food?
9 What colours were the flowers under the trees?
10 When did they get to the hills?
11 Was it hot in the cave?
12 Did Alex like the cave?
13 Who said, 'Do not tell anyone . . .'?

2 Where is Biff?

1 When did the children play games?
2 What was at the back of the cave?
3 What was full of stones?
4 Was there a big hole at the top of the stones?
5 Alex looked in the hole. What did he say?
6 What did the children take to the cave on Tuesday?
7 Catherine climbed on the stones. What did she see?
8 How did the children make the hole bigger?
9 Was the second cave dry?
10 Did Biff like the second cave?
11 Was the second cave smaller than the picnic cave?
12 Who says 'Where is Biff?'
13 Was Biff with Catherine?

14 Was Biff in the picnic cave?
15 What did the children shout?

3 In the dark passage

Choose the best answer.

1 Biff was (behind a stone/in a passage/in the picnic cave).
2 The passage was (not very high/very high/long).
3 The passage was (dry/wet).
4 The children heard a (quiet/loud) noise.
5 Alex cut his (face/arm/ankle).
6 The children found an old (cup/bone).
7 The children were (happy/unhappy).
8 The children (shouted/talked/listened).
9 The light from the torch was (white/red/yellow).
10 The children saw two (feet/ears/eyes).

4 Help

1 Did the animal close its eyes?
2 Was it an animal?
3 Did the children hear a loud noise?
4 Biff heard the noise. What did he do?
5 Who said, 'We can catch Biff outside'?
6 What was different in the wet cave?
7 Were the stones big or small?
8 Was there anybody outside?
9 Were Alex's feet hot?
10 Where was Biff?
11 Where did the children wait?
12 How many apples were in the bag?
13 How many blankets were in the bag?
14 Who was with grandfather?

5 The story of the cave

Finish the sentences:

1 The story was in the . . .
2 Lots of people . . . to the caves.
3 The story was on . . . too.
4 Dr. Vickers said the cave was very . . .
5 There were . . . pictures in the passage.
6 The stones were . . . and of stone.
7 People used small . . . for needles.
8 'Can we have a . . . ?' said Catherine.
9 'Yes, but do not go into any . . . ,' said grandmother.

The true story of the caves at Lascaux

1 When did the boys find the paintings at Lascaux?
2 Where is Lascaux?
3 When did people paint the pictures at Lascaux?
4 Are they pictures of dogs?
5 How did people see in the caves?
6 Are the paintings on the floor of the caves?
7 Are any of the pictures very big?
8 Did the people use green paint?
9 What colour are the lines?

Words in this book

an ankle   asleep   a bone   a cave

children   climb   cold   hot

a cloud   a cut   dark   light

dirty   down   up   a drink

drop	dry	wet	a face
fall	a fire	a hammer	heavy
high	a hill	a hole	kick
a knife	a newspaper	a noise	a nose

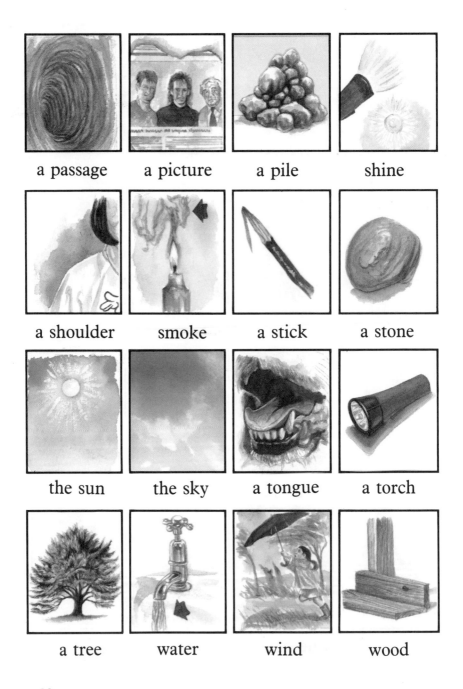

a passage   a picture   a pile   shine

a shoulder   smoke   a stick   a stone

the sun   the sky   a tongue   a torch

a tree   water   wind   wood

Start with English Readers

Grade 1
Po-Po
Mary and her Basket
Pat and her Picture
A New Tooth
The Kite

Grade 2
Peter and his Book
John and Paul go to School
The Bird and the Bread
Two Stories
Tonk and his Friends

Grade 3
Sam's Ball
The Fox and the Stork/The Bird and the Glass
The Big Race
The Man in the Big Car
The Queen's Handkerchief

Grade 4
Nine Stories About People
Four Clever People
In the Cave
An Apple for the Monkey

Grade 5
People and Things
Doctor Know It All/The Brave Little Tailor
The Flyer

Grade 6
The Bottle Imp
The World Around Us

Start with English Readers are also available on cassette.

Start with Words and Pictures

This alphabetical picture dictionary provides extra help for Grades 1 to 3. It
has been specially written for use with Start with English materials.

For practice using the words in the picture dictionary, there is the *Start with
Words, and Pictures Activity Book*.

Oxford University Press
Walton Street, Oxford OX2 6DP

Oxford New Tork Toronto
Petaling Jaya Singapore Hong Kong Tokyo
Delhi Bombay Calcutta Madras Karachi
Nairobi Dar es Salaam Cape Town
Melbourne Auckland

and associated companies in
Berlin Ibadan

ISBN 0 19 433791 X

First published 1988
Second impression 1989

Based on a syllabus devised by D H Howe

Illustrated by David Mitcheson

We would like to thank Ancient Art and Architecture Collection
for permission to reproduce photographs.

Printed in Hong Kong